20,000 Leagues Under the Sea

by Jules Verne

Abridged and adapted by Andrea M. Clare

Illustrated by David Grove

A PACEMAKER CLASSIC

GLOBE FEARON

Pearson Learning Group

Other Pacemaker Classics

The Adventures of Huckleberry Finn
The Adventures of Tom Sawyer
A Christmas Carol
Crime and Punishment
The Deerslayer
Dr. Jekyll and Mr. Hyde
Ethan Frome
Frankenstein
Great Expectations
Jane Eyre
The Jungle Book
The Last of the Mohicans
Moby Dick
The Moonstone
The Red Badge of Courage
Robinson Crusoe
The Scarlet Letter
A Tale of Two Cities
The Three Musketeers
The Time Machine
Treasure Island
Two Years Before the Mast
Wuthering Heights

ISBN 0-8224-9233-4
Printed in the United States of America

13 14 15   05 04

Globe
Fearon
Pearson Learning Group

1-800-321-3106
www.pearsonlearning.com

Contents

1 A Monster at Sea

Something strange was happening in 1866. People living near the sea told wild stories about a strange sea animal. Sailors were afraid to board their ships. People from countries around the world watched the sea.

For some time now, ships had been spotting a large sea animal. It was long and thin, much bigger than a whale. It was faster than any sea animal people had ever seen before. Sometimes it gave off a strange light. Sailors even saw the monster blow water 150 feet into the air.

No one knew what it was. Wild stories about shipwrecks were told in the news. A few ships ran into the monster. The monster knocked large holes in the ships' bottoms with its tail. Crossing the sea became very dangerous. Something had to be done. But no one seemed to know what could—or *should* —be done about it.

While all this was happening, I was visiting in America. My name is Professor Pierre Aronnax. I am Professor of Natural History at the National Museum, in France. My field is the sea, its plants and its animals. Like everyone else, I wondered what this monster could be.

Some people thought it was a floating island. But it moved too fast to be an island. Others believed it was a monster waiting to kill people at sea. A few people thought it was a "submarine," a ship that ran under the water. If so, was it being used for war?

I believed it could not be a submarine. In 1866, no country knew how to build such a submarine. And even if a country could build one, no one could hide it while it was being put together. Other countries would have found out about it. A strange sea monster was the only answer.

Many people had read my books about sea animals. Now they were asking for my thoughts about the sea monster. The *New York Herald* carried my answer: "The sea is deep. It hides many things. We do not know what animals can live ten miles under the water. Deep in the sea, water is very strong. It presses against animals so hard that few can live there. An animal must be very strong to take it. I believe that very large animals might live deep in the sea, animals we have never seen. After all, very large animals once walked on land. I believe that the monster is a giant whale."

My answer was read in papers across the country. I gave the world sound answers, not just wild stories. At last, governments of the world began to do something. The United States readied a ship to look for and kill the animal. The ship was the *Abraham Lincoln*. It waited in New York. When the monster was seen again, the ship would sail.

Then, in May, the monster was spotted in the South China Sea. Commander Farragut, captain of the *Abraham Lincoln*, sent me a letter:

"My dear Professor Aronnax,

If you would like to come with us on the *Abraham Lincoln* to hunt the monster, we would be pleased. A cabin has been made ready for you.

Commander Farragut"

Until this letter came, I had no thought of looking for this monster. But now, that one thought filled my head. I called to Conseil, my good friend. We always worked together.

"Conseil, let us get ready. We are going to hunt the sea monster!" I handed him the letter.

"It will be dangerous, Professor," he answered. "Commander Farragut will stop at nothing to kill it. We do not know where the hunt will take us."

"You are right," I said. "You do not have to come if you want to go back to France."

"I have no family, Professor. I would like to look for this monster."

3

We both got ready in a hurry, and boarded the *Abraham Lincoln* the next morning. Smoke was already coming from the ship. The captain was waiting for us.

"Commander Farragut, I am Professor Aronnax. This is my good friend, Conseil."

"I am happy to have you on board. We are now ready to begin our hunt. You may watch from the deck as we go out to sea."

With those words, the captain went to the engine room. The sailors let go the line. And the *Abraham Lincoln* began its dangerous hunt across the sea.

2 The Hunt

Soon we were far out in the Atlantic Ocean. Commander Farragut brought his men together on the deck. "We will kill the monster, or the monster will kill us," he said. "We will not let it get away. The ship carries cannons, guns, and harpoons. We also have the best harpooner around. His name is Ned Land."

The Captain pointed to a strong-looking man next to him. Ned Land was about 40 years old and was well over six feet tall. His strong arms looked like two tree trunks. He was holding a long harpoon in one hand. And we all could see that Ned Land knew well how to *use* that harpoon.

"To kill the animal, we must find it first," said the captain. "I will give $2,000 to the first man who spots the animal!"

"How are we going to find this monster, Captain?" Ned asked. "It keeps moving. It is spotted in the Pacific one week, and in the Atlantic the next."

"We will head for the Pacific and look for the animal near China," he answered. "That is where it was seen last. But we don't know where we might see it. It might even be close to us now."

For six weeks, every man kept his eyes on the sea. Every sailor wanted to be the first to spot the monster.

I stood watch near Ned Land. He was a quiet man most of the time. But when he was angry, his eyes filled with fire. And, as days went by, I had a feeling that our hunt for the monster was making him angry. Ned did not believe there was a monster.

"I have harpooned many whales," he said. "They were strong. But their tails could not break open the bottom of a ship. I have not seen this monster with my own eyes. Until I do, I will not believe it lives."

After ten weeks in the Atlantic, we went around Cape Horn. We were in the Pacific Ocean at last!

On July 20, 1867 we were near the South China Sea. The sailors were happy. They believed we would soon spot the monster. The men would not eat. They could not sleep. They did almost nothing but watch the sea. A few times each day, we thought we saw the monster. Our eyes were beginning to play tricks on us. The monster was never there.

For 12 weeks the *Abraham Lincoln* sailed around the Pacific. We saw nothing—only the sea. The men grew tired. Commander Farragut pushed them on. If he had not, the men would have turned the ship around. They did not believe in the monster anymore. But even the captain could not stop the bad feelings of the men. At last he told them, "Let us look for three more days. If we do not see the monster, we will go back home." These words made the sailors feel better.

Two days went by. We tried to trick the animal. We pulled meat in our wake. If the monster was hungry, it might come after the meat. But still we saw nothing.

One more day of this and we would have to turn back. That evening, I was talking with Conseil on the deck of the ship. "Tomorrow we will go home again," I said.

"Yes, Professor. It is too bad that we did not find your giant whale."

We stopped talking and listened to the quiet waves splashing against the ship. Then the quiet of the night ended. Ned Land's voice roared out. "I can see it! There it is! *I see the monster!*"

3 A Strange Kind of Whale

Ned's cry brought us all running. He was pointing into the dark night. All was black and still. I wondered how Ned could see anything. We all looked where Ned was pointing. Then we saw it!

All at once, about 1,200 feet away, the sea seemed to catch on fire. Deep in the water there was a bright light. It was long and round like the monster! And it was moving our way! "It is coming straight at us!" I cried.

"Stop engines! Back up!" called Commander Farragut. The ship moved away from the light.

The monster came at us again, but it did not attack. It seemed to be playing. It went around our ship. Then it went away. All at once, it came toward us again. It was moving faster than any sea animal I had ever seen. It was going to attack!

But just before it was about to hit the ship, the light went out. We waited for the blow. It did not come. Then, we saw the light shining on the other side of our ship! Had it gone under our ship or around it? We did not know.

"All engines full!" cried the captain. "Get this ship out of here."

I was standing beside the captain. "I don't believe what is happening," I said. "We are running away from this monster, not attacking."

Commander Farragut turned to face me. "I do not know what this monster is," he said. "I will not put us in danger until I must. Tomorrow morning, when we can see this animal, we will attack. Not before then."

The monster followed us all night long. No one on board thought of sleeping. We watched the bright light deep in the water behind us. Then, about one o'clock, the light went out. We could not see the animal. Was it still there?

We soon found out. We heard the sound of water blowing high in the air. Ned Land was standing near me. "That is the sound a whale makes, Professor. But I have never heard a whale this loud."

All night, the crew got ready for the attack. Guns were put in place. Ned readied his harpoon.

At six o'clock, the sun came up. We saw the monster a mile away. The long, black animal was resting on top of the waves.

"Full speed!" called Commander Farragut. "Begin the attack!"

As we turned to attack, the monster began to blow water into the air. And it started to move away from us.

We followed the monster all day. We soon
learned that we could not catch it. It was faster
than we were. The Commander pushed the ship
until we felt it shake.

"The ship might blow up at these speeds," I
said to him.

"I know," he answered. "What else can we do?
If we keep pressing it, it may get tired."

But the animal did not get tired. At last, the Commander said to his men, "This is as close as we can get. Fire the guns!"

The first cannon roared. But the shell fell short. The next one hit the monster right on the back. The men watched in surprise. The shell rolled off the monster's back and splashed into the sea. Even guns could not hurt this strange whale.

The monster kept on moving away from us. We could not catch up with it. Soon it was too far away to fire at. Then it was gone. We did not spot it any more that day.

Night fell. We kept on looking for the monster. Then, at ten o'clock, we saw the light in the water again.

Ned Land went over to Commander Farragut. "The animal is not moving," he said. "It seems to be asleep. If we can get close enough, I will harpoon it."

"Then get ready with your harpoon," Commander Farragut answered.

The *Abraham Lincoln* moved toward the sleeping whale. When we were 100 feet away, the captain cut the engines. All was quiet now. We floated toward the strange animal.

I could see Ned holding his harpoon. Now we were only 20 feet away. All at once, Ned threw the harpoon with all his might. It hit the animal right on its back!

A deep ringing sound filled the air. The light in the water went out. Then I heard a loud noise. The monster was blowing water into the air again. The water blew all over the ship. It knocked men to the deck. Then the ship was jarred by a heavy blow. The blow threw me over the side. I fell into the sea!

4 Lost and Alone

I was going down, down! The water was so deep! There was no bottom. I pushed against the water with my hands. I tried to swim. At last, I came back up to the surface.

I looked around me for the ship. It was ten o'clock, and the night was very dark. Far away, I could just make out something black. It was moving away from me. It was the *Abraham Lincoln!*

Did Conseil know that I had been knocked over the side? Would anyone turn back to save me? "Help! *Help!*" I cried. I tried to swim toward the ship, but my clothes were too heavy. My shoes pulled at my feet. I was lost!

"Help!" I called again. A wave washed over my head. My mouth filled with water. I started to go down again. This was the end.

All at once, something pulled at my clothes. I was being pulled to the surface! Then I heard Conseil's voice.

"If you would hold my arm, we will swim together," he said.

"It is you, Conseil! Thank God! But how did you get here? Did that blow throw you into the sea, too?"

"No, Professor. I saw you being washed away. So I jumped after you. I am your friend, and I wanted to help you."

"What about the ship?" I asked him. "Do you think it will come back for us?"

"I don't think so, Professor. The monster knocked a hole in our ship. It will float, but I don't think it can turn around."

"Then we are lost!" I said.

"Don't give up, Professor. They may send a small boat to look for us, if we hold out until morning. They can't look for us in the dark."

It would be a long time until morning. We thought of a plan. One of us would float on his back while the other would swim. In this way, we could help each other. One of us would rest every ten minutes.

"It will help us to float if we take our shoes off," said Conseil. "And let's take off our heavy clothes."

We swam for a long time. The water was very cold. I was becoming more and more tired. "I don't think I can make it," I said. "I am too tired to swim."

"Hold on," Conseil said. "What was that?"

"Did you hear something?"

"Yes, I think I heard a voice," he answered. "*Help!*" he cried. "*Help!*"

Far off, a voice answered. "Over here!" the voice called.

Conseil pulled me toward the sound. "I am too cold and too tired," I said. "I can't make it." My head went under the water. But Conseil would not let me go. He kept swimming toward the voice we had heard.

Then, at last, my arm hit something hard. I felt a hand hold me and pull me up. "Come on up, Professor," the voice said.

I knew who it was! "Ned Land!" I cried. "What a surprise! Am I ever happy to see you!"

"And I have another surprise for you, Professor," he said. "You will never guess what it is. We are sitting on your giant whale!"

"You are joking," I said. I felt the animal with my hand. "I don't believe it! This is not an animal! It is too cold and too hard. It is iron. This must be some kind of submarine!"

"Then it must have men on board," said Conseil.

"Yes," answered Ned. "But I have been resting here for a long time. If it is a submarine, it must have a hatch. I have not found one. All I have found are these iron rings on the top. And I have not heard any sounds."

"If the submarine stays on the surface until morning," said Conseil, "we might find a way to get inside."

Just then, the submarine began to move.

"Hold the rings!" I called. "Don't fall off!"

The submarine raced across the top of the water. Our dangerous ride lasted until the sun came up. Then, at first light the submarine started to dive under the water!

"It is all over now!" cried Ned. "Make as much noise as you can! If the people inside hear us, they may let us in."

We began to bang on the top of the ship. We made as much noise as we could. All at once, the submarine stopped. We heard a loud noise inside. A hatch opened near us, and seven men came out. The men did not say anything. Without a word, they just picked us up and threw us inside the strange submarine.

5 Prisoners

The hatch closed behind us. We could feel the submarine beginning to dive again. The men pushed us into a small room. They closed the door, and we heard something slide across it. Everything was dark. We were alone.

"What is going to happen to us now?" asked Ned.

"What will they do with us?" asked Conseil.

"Let's wait and see," I answered. "We should know very soon."

Time went by. We could not see or hear anything. Then, all at once, the lights came on. The door opened and two men came in.

One man was a sailor. The other man was the captain of the ship. The captain had black eyes that seemed to look inside us. He was not a tall man, but he was strong, and he stood very straight.

The two men took a careful look at us. Then, they began talking to each other. We did not understand a word of what they were saying.

"Let us out of here," said Ned. He was beginning to get angry. "Let us out. We don't belong here. We want to go back to our ship! You knocked us into the sea. We held anything that floated.

Let me tell you what happened." Ned tried to tell the strange men our story.

"I don't think they understand English," I said. "Let me tell them our story in French." When I finished, the men still did not seem to know what we were saying.

"Let me try," said Conseil. He told our story in German. When Conseil finished, the two men turned around and left the room.

"How do you like that!" said Ned. "They did not understand a word. *Now* what are we going to do?"

"I don't know," I answered. "We must find a way to talk with them."

Just then, the door opened. A sailor came into the room. He brought us dry clothes and food. He set the table with beautiful covered dishes. Then he left, without saying a word. We tried to talk to him but he would not answer.

Ned was still angry, but the food was making him feel better.

"Smell that food!" he said. "It smells great! What is it?"

"It looks like fish," answered Conseil. "There are so many kinds!"

"This ship must have a good cook," I said.

We sat down and ate our dinner. The food was as good as it smelled.

"I am very full," said Ned as he finished one of the bowls. "I guess things will turn out all right. They would not feed us and then kill us."

"The captain must be a good man," I said. "But let's talk about it tomorrow. I am very tired. I cannot keep my eyes open."

Soon, we were all sound asleep. We must have been asleep for a long time. When we woke up, the air in our room was almost gone.

"How do they bring fresh air into the submarine when it is under the water?" I wondered. Soon, I felt the submarine begin to move up. I knew we had come to the surface again. Before long, I could smell the sea air. It was coming into our room through a small hole over the door.

The fresh air woke Ned and Conseil up.

"Fresh air?" asked Ned. "Where is it coming from?"

"We are on the surface again," I answered. "The hatches are open, and the ship is filling up with fresh air."

"The sea air is making me hungry," said Ned. "I wonder when they will bring us breakfast."

"It should be soon," answered Conseil. "I wonder what they will feed us today."

We waited for a while, but no one came.

"Do you think we will be prisoners in this room from now on?" Ned asked.

"I don't know," I answered. "If the captain wants to hide his submarine from the world, we will be. But if he cares about our lives, he will let us go."

"I don't think he wants the world to know about the submarine," said Conseil.

"No, and I don't think he cares about our lives," Ned said. "He will kill us or keep us prisoners. Just the thought of it makes me angry! I will not be shut up in a cage like a wild animal. If I can't fish and hunt, I will go out of my head!"

Ned's eyes were beginning to fill with fire. "No man can keep me here! I will break out! I will kill them before they kill me!"

All at once, we heard the sliding noise at our door. Ned hurried toward it. The door opened, and a sailor came in. Ned jumped on him and put his hands around the man's neck! Conseil and I tried to stop him. We were afraid Ned would kill him. Then we heard another voice.

"Stop, Ned Land! Ned, Professor Aronnax, Conseil, please listen to me."

Ned let go of the man. We all looked up. The captain of the submarine was standing at the door. And he was talking to us in English!

"Professor, don't let me surprise you. I can talk in French, English, or German," he said. "I wanted to hear your stories before I did anything. How strange it is that I have you on board. I know of your work, Professor. I have read your books about the sea."

"What are you going to do with us?" I asked.

"You have made things hard for me," he answered. "I don't want to be a part of the outside world. We have our own world on this ship. We don't need anyone else. Until now, no one on land knew about our submarine. If we let you go, they will find out."

What had these men done that made them hide from other men? Were they planning a war? Were they running away from something they had done?

And what was to happen to us? Now that we knew about the submarine, would the captain kill us?

"I know what you are wondering," the captain said. "I will tell you my plans. You and your friends will live. But you will not set foot on land again. You will be prisoners on this submarine."

"For how long?" I asked.

"From now on," the captain answered.

"In this room?" I asked. "In this one small room?"

"No, you may walk through the ship. You may go on deck. You may use anything on the ship that you want. There is a lot to see and learn on this ship. Professor, even you will learn new things about the sea. You will get used to being here. You may even begin to like being on board."

"What is the catch, Captain?" Ned asked. "What do you ask of us?"

"There is no catch, Mr. Land," he answered. "I ask only one thing. Once in a while, there will be things going on that I don't want you to see. I will ask all of you to come back to this room and stay here."

"But we want to see our friends again," I said. "And if we learn more about the sea, we will want to tell the world. We are not sailors like you and your men, Captain. We don't want to stay on this submarine."

"I understand how you feel, Professor. But I did not ask you to come on board. You and your friends attacked this ship. Now you ask that we save you. It is our lives or yours, Professor. You may stay here as prisoners, or we will have to kill you. There is no other way."

6 The *Nautilus*

"There is only one answer we can give," I said. "We must go along with the captain if we want to live."

"You are right, Professor," said Conseil.

"You may be right, but I still don't like it," said Ned. He turned to face the captain. "Let me tell you this, Captain. I will try to get away when the right time comes. You will not keep me here for long!"

"You may try to get away, *but you will never make it*," answered the captain. We were all quiet for a minute. Then the captain went on. "Now that we understand each other, let me tell you who I am. My name is Captain Nemo. This submarine that will be your new home is the *Nautilus*."

Captain Nemo went to the door and called out to one of his men. A sailor came into the room, carrying food. "I am sure you must be hungry," the captain said. "This food is for Ned and Conseil. Professor Aronnax, you will come with me."

I followed Captain Nemo through the submarine to a large room. In the room was one long table. Around it were many chairs. The table was set with beautiful dishes. The walls were covered with fine paintings. It was hard to believe that there could be such a room in a submarine.

Captain Nemo pointed to a chair at the head of the table. "Please sit down," he said.

As we ate our lunch, Captain Nemo told me how the food was made. "Most of these dishes are new to you," he said. "All of our food comes from the sea."

"But this seems to be meat, not fish," I said, pointing to one dish. "What is it, Captain Nemo?"

"That is turtle," he said. "The other dish you just finished was shark meat."

"And what about the vegetables?" I asked.

"The vegetables are plants from the sea. Your drink was whale milk. But the sea gives us more than just food, Professor. It dresses us, too. On the *Nautilus*, everything we use—even our clothes —comes from the sea!"

"You really love the sea, don't you, Captain?"

"Yes, I love the sea. The sea is everything. And I love the *Nautilus*. She is a beautiful ship. If you are finished eating, Professor, I would like to show you around."

I followed the captain into the next room. It was filled with books.

"Captain Nemo, you have so many books!"

"There are 12,000 in this room," he answered. "These books are my only tie to the outside world. You may use them, Professor. Anything you might want to read is here."

"Thank you," I answered. "I will look through them sometime."

From here, we went into the drawing room. An organ rested against one wall. Near it were four small paintings.

"The paintings are beautiful," I said.

"You may know some of them," answered the captain.

"Yes, here is a Raphael, and this is a Leonardo da Vinci!"

Then, something else caught my eye. There were
many small tables in the room. Each one was
covered with shells.

"Where did you get these beautiful shells?" I asked. "You have sea stars and feather stars! And look at this garden of pearls!"

"Do you like them, Professor? I am very pleased with them, too. I found them on the bottom of the sea. The pink pearls came from the Red Sea. I found the green and blue ones in the Atlantic Ocean. I picked the yellow and black ones from the floor of the Pacific. But this is the one I like best."

The captain pointed to a large white pearl. It was bigger than a hen's egg. "There are more like this," he said. "Some are even bigger. I will show them to you some time. Now, follow me. I want to show you the rest of the ship."

We went down the hall. The captain stopped at a door. "This will be your cabin, Professor."

So far, all the cabins I had seen were in the front part of the ship. Now we went toward the back. We went by Ned's and Conseil's cabin. Then we saw the kitchen and the bath. The door leading to the sailors' cabins was closed, so I could not see them. I still did not know how many men were on board the *Nautilus*.

Next, the captain took me through the engine room. "The *Nautilus* runs on electricity," he said. "We make electricity from the water around us. It gives us our speed and our light. It does most of the heavy work on the ship."

"No wonder you are so pleased with the ship."

"Yes, Professor," he answered. "I love the *Nautilus* as if it were my own child. There is no danger on this ship. Fire will not hurt it, because it is made of iron, not wood. Wind will not roll it, even in heavy seas. All we have to do is dive. The sea is quiet a few feet under the water. I made the plans for this submarine, and I helped build it. Yes, I am pleased with this ship, Professor!"

"But how did you build it without the world finding out?" I asked.

"Parts of the ship were sent to me and my men from all over the world. We made sure that no two parts came from the same place. And no two parts were sent to the same name. Then, we found a place where no one would find us. My friends and I put it together there. We left nothing behind us, so no one will ever know we were there."

"But you must have had a lot of money to build the ship," I said.

"I do, Professor. I have more money than you could ever guess. My money, too, comes from the sea. But now, I must get back to work. We are near Japan. If you like, you can watch our travels from the drawing room."

I went back to the drawing room, deep in thought. Who was this strange man? Was he good or bad? What was he up to? I had no answers.

As I sat there thinking, Ned and Conseil came in. I told them about everything I had seen. I told them about the shells, the books, and the pearls. "I don't care about those things," Ned roared in an angry voice. "How many men are on the *Nautilus?* We need to know that before we try to escape."

"I don't know, Ned," I answered. "But this ship is better than any ship ever made before. I would like to learn more about it, before we escape."

Just then, the lights in the drawing room went out. The room was dark. We heard the sound of something sliding across the wall.

All at once, we could see out. The wall had opened up. We were standing in front of a large window, looking into the sea. All around us, the water was filled with fish and other sea animals.

"How beautiful!" I said. "I have never seen so many fish. What beautiful colors they are!"

"How strange! How very strange!" said Ned. For once, he did not have anything else to say. We could not take our eyes off the window. I don't know how long we sat there watching. It was a long time. Then the wall closed over the window. The lights came back on inside the drawing room. We went back to our rooms for dinner. Soon after dinner, we fell asleep. There was something about the food we ate that always made us sleepy.

7 The Woods of the Isle of Crespo

For the next five days, we did not see Captain Nemo. The wall in the drawing room was closed, and we could not see out. It almost seemed that Ned, Conseil, and I were alone on the ship. The sailors stayed in the back part of the ship. They kept their door closed.

Every morning, the *Nautilus* came to the surface to fill up with fresh air. When it did, I climbed through the hatch and stood on the deck. Each morning, I watched the same sailor come to the deck and look around. He took a reading on the sun, and then went back inside. He was the only sailor that we saw.

We began to believe that we would never see Captain Nemo again. Then, on November 16, I walked into my room with Ned and Conseil. There was a note on my table.

"Professor Aronnax:

Tomorrow morning a hunting party will be held in the woods of the Isle of Crespo. You and your friends may come along.

The Commander of the *Nautilus*,
Captain Nemo"

"A hunt!" said Ned. "And in the woods of the Isle of Crespo!"

"It looks like we are going to be on land!" cried Conseil.

"We must go!" cried Ned. "Once we are on land, we can escape!"

"We must see the Isle of Crespo first," I said. "It could be very small. It might be miles away from people."

Ned looked at me, but he did not say anything. He was deep in thought. Was he planning an escape? At last, he said, "It is late. Tomorrow we will have a lot to do. Let's get some sleep. Good night."

"Good night," we answered.

Early the next morning, Ned, Conseil, and I went into the drawing room. Captain Nemo was waiting for us.

"We would like to go hunting with you, Captain," I said. "But how can you hunt in these woods? You told us you would never go on land again."

"These are my woods," he answered. "There are no bears, no tigers, no deer. These woods are not on land. My woods grow under the sea!"

"Then how can we hunt?" Ned asked. "Guns will not work under the water, and we will have no air!"

"Your guns will work with electricity," he answered. "And you will carry air in a tank on your back!"

"I am staying here!" said Ned. "Who wants to hunt under the water? This is no hunting party!" Ned was angry. His plan of escape would have to wait. The woods that he thought would hide us were at the bottom of the sea.

Ned went back to his room. Conseil and I followed the captain into a small tank room. We put on our diving suits and air tanks. The captain gave each of us a gun. Then, the tank room filled up with water. When it was full, the captain opened a hatch.

We stepped out on the floor of the sea! It was a beautiful garden of colors. The sun was shining on the waves high over our heads. Schools of fish were swimming around us.

We walked for a long time. Then, Captain Nemo stopped and pointed to some tall plants in front of us. With our diving suits on, we could not talk to each other.

These must be the woods of the Isle of Crespo! I thought. *The sea plants are as tall as trees. They grow straight up toward the sun.*

We walked into the woods. The plants were all around us. After a while, we came to a hill. It was made of large rocks. The top of the hill went up to the surface. It was out of the water. Dry land was only a few steps in front of us now.

The captain stopped. This is as far as we would go. Captain Nemo would not go too near the land.

Over our heads, we could see sea lions swimming and playing on the surface of the water. They did not see us. The captain fired his gun and killed one of them. The sea lion fell to the bottom. A sailor walked over and picked the animal up. Then we moved on.

Soon, we saw a large bird flying over our heads. It was in the air, diving toward the water. One of the sailors fired, just as the bird was going to catch a fish. The bird fell like a rock to the bottom, where the sailor picked it up.

We hunted most of the day. Then Captain Nemo pointed toward the ship. It was time to go back. It was late afternoon, and the walk would take until dark.

I was walking behind the captain. All at once, he turned around and pushed me down. The captain threw himself to the sand beside me.

I looked up. There, over our heads, were two large sharks. Their mouths were so big they could cut a man in two! They were coming right at us! Had they seen us?

We lay still. The sharks did not see us. But one came so close that it hit me with its tail as it went by.

The sharks moved on, and we got back up. Soon, we were back at the *Nautilus*. "Ned, you should have come!" cried Conseil. "It was beautiful!"

"And dangerous," I said. "Thank you for saving us from the sharks, Captain."

"Sharks?" asked Ned. As soon as he heard the story, he wished he had come. "The next time, I will go, too. And I'll take my harpoon."

The next morning, I went up on deck. The sailor I saw there every morning was looking over the sea. Other sailors were pulling in fishing lines.

Captain Nemo came out and took a reading of the sun. When he finished, he turned to me. I could see that he wanted to talk.

"Look at the sea, Professor," he said. "It is like a living friend. Sometimes it is happy. Sometimes it is angry. Last night, it fell asleep just as we did. This morning, it is waking up before our eyes. The sea is a living thing, filled with living things. Some people say that the sea kills men.

But it also helps animals live—animals *and me!* I sometimes think the sea is my only friend."

Once he said this to me, the captain went down the hatch. I followed him down and went to the drawing room. Soon, the *Nautilus* began moving.

Weeks went by before we saw Captain Nemo again. And we saw very little of Ned. He was keeping to himself. Ned felt like a caged animal. He could not stand being closed in. All he could think about was escaping from the *Nautilus*.

Conseil and I were together a lot. The window of the drawing room was open for a while each day. Conseil helped me take notes on the fish and other sea animals that we saw. Captain Nemo was right. I was beginning to like living on the *Nautilus*.

"I am glad the window is open," I said. "I could sit here watching the sea and never get tired."

"No wonder Captain Nemo loves it so," said Conseil. "Each day I see a plant or fish that I have never seen before."

"I wish Ned would watch with us," I said.

"He wants to be alone, Professor," said Conseil. "He is tired of being a prisoner. Ned loves the sea as a harpooner. He can't harpoon whales on the *Nautilus*. Ned does not like to learn about fish the way we do."

"He wants to escape as much as I want to stay here," I said.

Just then we stopped talking. We saw something strange outside the window. A ship was going down. We could see the sinking ship heading for the bottom. We could even see sailors caught in the ship's ropes. But there was nothing we could do. It was too late to save them. I wondered if anyone else knew—or cared—about what was happening.

We saw many shipwrecks after that. But we did not see Captain Nemo until January 18. When we did see him, strange things began to happen.

We were in the South Pacific, near the Galapagos Islands. That morning I went on deck as I always did. The same sailor came up and looked around the sea. He called out, and Captain Nemo came on deck right away.

The captain looked at the sea. His face became cold. All at once, he turned on me. "Get back to your cabin. Take your friends with you!" he cried.

"But why, Captain?" I asked.

"Do as you are told. You are not to see what happens here. I told you when you first came on board . . ."

The captain did not finish his words. The sailor pushed me down the hatch.

8 The Coral Kingdom

We were prisoners again, housed together in one room. We did not know why, but the lights in our room had been turned off. At last, a sailor brought us our breakfast. The lights came on again.

"What are they afraid we will see?" Ned asked. "What are they up to?"

"I don't know," I answered, "but something strange is happening. I have never seen the captain so angry."

"We might as well eat," Conseil said. "We may be here a long time."

Before we finished our food, we began to feel strange.

"My eyes will not stay open," Conseil told us.

"I am very sleepy," Ned said in a quiet voice. "The room seems to be falling over."

"They put something in our food!" I cried. "They want us to sleep. What is it they don't want us to hear?"

We were too tired to say any more. Soon we fell asleep. We were asleep for a long time. When I woke up, it was the next morning.

I looked around the room. Ned and Conseil were gone. My door was open.

The sailors must have moved them back to their cabin, I thought.

I went down the hall and looked in their cabin. Ned and Conseil were both still sleeping. I walked to the drawing room and went in.

Captain Nemo was there! He looked tired. His eyes were red.

He must have been up all night, I thought.

The captain kept walking across the room. He seemed to be deep in thought. He did not look at all happy.

At last, the captain saw me. At first, he looked surprised. Then he said to me, "Will you help me, Professor?"

"What is it?" I asked.

"One of my men is sick. I have tried everything I know. Is there anything you can do?" he asked.

"I don't know." I said. "I will be glad to help, if I can."

"Then follow me."

The captain took me to a cabin near the back of the ship. A sailor was resting on a bed. He was not sick. He had been hurt. The man had a bad blow on his head.

"What happened to him?" I asked.

"That does not matter!" the captain answered. "He was hurt trying to save another sailor from danger, The man was his friend. On the *Nautilus*, a man will do anything for a friend. We are all brothers here!"

The captain stood over the sailor. "Do you think he will make it?" he asked.

"No," I answered. "Nothing can save him now."

"Then, please, go away," the captain told me.

As I left the room, I could hear the captain crying.

I did not see the captain again until the next morning. I went on deck as I always did. Captain Nemo was there.

He came up to me. "Would you like to go for a walk today?" he asked.

"With my friends?"

"Yes," he answered. "We are in the Coral Sea. We are going to the Coral Kingdom. Go put your diving suits on."

Soon, Ned, Conseil, and I were ready to go. We met Captain Nemo in the tank room. About ten other sailors were with him. Three of the men were carrying a long roll of white cloth. The room filled up with water, and we stepped out of the hatch.

The shining surface of the sea was far above us. In front of us, I could see the Coral Kingdom. The Kingdom was made up of many small coral animals. These small animals grow on top of each other until they look like rocks.

We walked between these coral rocks for a long time. At last, we came to an open place. There were small hills all over the sand. At one side, there was a cross made of coral.

Captain Nemo pointed to the sand near the cross. The sailors walked over to it and began to dig.

All at once, I knew what was happening! *The men are burying their friend*, I thought. *This is their beautiful last resting place under the sea!*

After the sailor was placed in the ground, he was covered with sand. Shells and coral were placed over the new little hill. The men bowed their heads. Then we went back to the ship.

That evening, I sat in the drawing room. Captain Nemo came in and sat down. "Our friend is resting with his brothers," he said. "He rests in a quiet place."

"He is safe from sharks," I said.

"Yes, he is safe from sharks," he answered. "And from men!"

The strange happenings of the last two days made me wonder about the captain again. I was seeing a new side of the man. He cared very much for his own men, almost like a father. At the same time, he was very angry at men in the outside world. I wondered again why the captain had put us asleep. What did he want us to keep from seeing or hearing? Had he attacked a ship? Had the sailor from the *Nautilus* been killed in the attack? I could only guess.

For the next week, the *Nautilus* traveled through the Indian Ocean. On January 28, 1868 we were near Ceylon. Something happened here that again threw a new light on Captain Nemo.

9 Diving for Pearls

We were looking out the window at the floor of the sea off Ceylon. Captain Nemo came in.

"When you first came on this ship, you saw my pearls," Captain Nemo said. "I told you there were many more like them. We are near the best oyster beds in the world. Would you like to see them?"

"Yes!" we said.

"We are here early," the captain went on. "In March, men will come here to dive for the pearls. As many as 300 boats may come. But there is no one here now."

"The water is deep," Conseil said. "How do the men swim to the bottom before they run out of air?"

"The men hold a heavy stone between their feet," the captain answered. "The rock pulls them down in a hurry. They stay under the water only a short time, not even a minute. Before they have to come up for air, they can fill a basket with oysters."

"That sounds like dangerous work," said Ned. "Do they get much pay?"

"Only pennies," answered the captain. "The men they work for keep all the pearls. And there is always the danger of sharks."

"Sharks!" we cried.

"Yes," he answered. "But when we visit the oyster beds, each of us will have a knife. If you still want to go, we will begin early tomorrow morning."

"Sharks or no sharks, we want to come along."

The next morning we went to the tank room and put on our diving suits. The room filled with water and Captain Nemo opened the hatch. We stepped out on to the sea floor. Each of us had a knife because of the danger of sharks. But Ned Land was carrying a large harpoon.

It was a long walk to the oyster beds. But, at last, we got there. On the sea floor in front of us there were oysters everywhere—as far as we could see.

I thought Captain Nemo would stop when we got to the oyster beds. But he kept on walking. Where was he taking us?

Then, I saw it. In front of us, there was a hill of rocks. There was a large hole in one of these rocks. The captain went into the hole. We followed. Deep inside this opening, we could see a large oyster. It was more than seven feet wide!

The shell was open. The captain placed his knife along the side so it could not shut. With his hand, he then moved a covering inside the animal. There before us was a pearl as large as an orange!

How beautiful! I thought. *So this is how Captain Nemo gets his money from the sea!*

I wanted to feel it with my hand, but the captain waved me away. Then, I knew what he was planning to do. Captain Nemo was growing this beautiful pearl. Some day he would take it from the sea, but not today.

Captain Nemo picked up his knife. We followed him back to the oyster beds. As we were walking, the captain tapped me and pointed. We stopped.

Just a few feet in front of us, an Indian man was diving for pearls. He held a stone between his feet. He had come to dive early. No one else would come to dive for another five weeks.

We watched this man for a long time. We saw him dive, fill his basket with oysters, and swim back to the top. He did this over and over again. The man did not see us. He did not know we were there, in our diving suits, watching him.

We watched him pick up oysters on the bottom. All at once, the Indian looked up. His face fell. Then, we saw it. A few feet over his head, there was a giant shark! It was more than 25 feet long. And it was coming at him! The large mouth was open. We could see row after row of shining, white teeth.

The man tried to swim away. Just as the shark opened his mouth to cut the man in two, the Indian rolled to one side. The shark missed him, but its tail knocked him to the bottom.

The shark turned around. It went for the Indian again!

Captain Nemo moved in to help. He went straight for the shark with his knife. The shark saw the captain and turned on him.

The captain pulled away just as the monster fish attacked. As the shark slid by, Captain Nemo pushed his knife deep into the shark's side. The water began turning red. The shark was hurt, but it kept attacking. The captain held on to the animal, trying to kill him. He cut the shark again and again with his knife.

But the shark was strong. It rolled and knocked Captain Nemo over with its tail. Then it turned around and came back ready to cut the captain in two! I could see the white rows of teeth in its mouth.

All at once, Ned was there. He moved toward the shark with his harpoon. Ned pushed the harpoon deep into the animal. The water turned deep red. It was all over! Ned had killed the monster shark!

Captain Nemo got up. He went over to the Indian and picked him up. Carrying him in his arms, the captain swam to the surface. We helped the captain put the man in a fishing boat there. We stayed with the Indian until he opened his eyes. We could see that he was all right.

"Take these," the captain said to the surprised man. He had never seen men in diving suits before. The captain took a bag of pearls from his pocket. He put them in the Indian's hand. The Indian was more surprised than ever.

Then the captain turned to us. "Thank you, Ned," he said. "Without your help the shark would have killed me for sure. Let us go back now."

Once we were on the *Nautilus*, we talked with the captain.

"Why did you save that man?" I asked. "He is part of that world you are running from."

"No, Professor," the captain answered. "I do not run from the poor. I do not run from the sick. I do not run from those who have lost everything because of war. No, Professor, I do not run from such people. I know how much they have been hurt. They are my brothers."

10 The South Pole

From Ceylon, we sailed to the Red Sea. From the Red Sea, we traveled to the Mediterranean.

"Now we can escape!" Ned said to us. "The time has come!"

"As soon as we are close to land," Conseil told him.

"And as soon as the *Nautilus* travels on the surface," I said.

But the captain kept the ship away from land. When land was near, he traveled under the water. By late February, we had crossed into the North Atlantic. We crossed the Equator and kept traveling south. We traveled south for more than three weeks.

"Where are we going now?" Ned asked.

"We are heading south," I answered. "It looks like we are heading for Antarctica. That is all I know."

Conseil joked with Ned. "We will stop sometime," he laughed. "If we keep going south, we will hit an iceberg or something!"

Now that we were on the open sea, the *Nautilus* traveled on the surface of the water. There were no other ships around that might spot us.

The three of us were sitting on the deck one morning. It was a beautiful March day. "Look!" Ned called to us. "Whales! There must be 50 whales out there!"

"They have come south to escape from man," I said. "So many are hunted in the North Atlantic that few are left."

"If only I could harpoon one!" Ned cried. "Look how close they are coming to the *Nautilus!*"

Conseil answered, "Why not ask the captain? He might let you hunt them."

Conseil did not have time to finish. Ned ran off to find the captain.

In a few minutes, Captain Nemo came on deck. He looked around and watched the whales playing.

"Captain, may I hunt them—just one?" Ned asked.

"What good would it do?" the captain answered. "We will not use the meat or fat. So why kill it? We do not kill animals just to kill them. Already, too few whales are left. No, Ned, you may not hunt these whales."

From that day on, Ned was angry with the captain.

On March 14, we saw pieces of ice on the water. On March 16, ice was all around us. "We have crossed the Antarctic Circle," I said. "I wonder how far he is planning to go."

"He will have to stop soon," answered Conseil.

"I am not so sure."

By night, the *Nautilus* was breaking the ice fields in front of us. But soon, the ice was too strong. The *Nautilus* could not move. The ship could not break the ice in front of it.

The captain came into the drawing room. "We are trapped," I said to him.

He laughed. "Professor, we are not trapped. The *Nautilus* will break out and go even more to the south. We are going to the South Pole!"

"But how, Captain?" I asked. "Will we put wings on the *Nautilus* and fly over the ice?"

"Fly, Professor?" he asked. "You still do not believe in the *Nautilus*. No, we will not fly over it. We will go under it. But, we cannot come up for air until we are in open sea. There should be open sea at the Pole. We should be there in three days."

Soon, the submarine was diving under the ice field. The next day, we were 4,000 feet under the water.

The *Nautilus* began to slow down. Soon, the submarine began to float toward the surface. Then I felt a blow.

"We have hit the bottom of the ice field," I said.

"But we are 3,000 feet under water!" Conseil said.

"Then there is 4,500 feet of ice over us," I answered. "For every foot of ice above the water, there are two feet under the water. The ice sticks up 1,500 feet into the air."

All day long, the *Nautilus* bumped against the bottom of the ice. By dinner time, we were only 1,000 feet under the surface. The ice was getting thin. Next morning, we had only 150 feet to go.

At last, the captain came into the drawing room. "We are here," he said. "Come, look at the open sea!"

We hurried to the deck. Water was all around us. The air was almost warm. Birds flew over our heads. Fish jumped in the water. A few icebergs floated near us.

"Are we at the South Pole?" I asked.

"I don't know for sure," Captain Nemo answered. "We will take a reading at noon."

About ten miles south of us, we could see land. "We will take our reading from there," the captain told us.

When the *Nautilus* got near the land, we set out in a small boat. We were soon there. Conseil started to get out.

"Wait!" I said. "No man has ever been here before. Captain Nemo should be the first to set foot on the ground."

"Thank you," the captain answered.

He jumped from the boat. A smile covered his face.

All around us, the land and ice were covered with animals. There were birds and bears and sea lions—even sea elephants. They did not run away from us.

"They have not learned to be afraid of man," I said.

"I am glad Ned is not with us," Conseil said. "He would want to hunt these beautiful animals."

The captain walked in front of us. "The sun will tell us if we are at the South Pole," he said. "If the sun sets at noon, we are at the Pole!"

The captain took a sun-sighting wheel out of a bag. "It is almost time," he said. "I will watch the sun through this. Professor, please tell me when it is 12 o'clock."

We watched the sun begin to set.

"Noon!" I cried.

"The South Pole!" he answered. The captain pulled out a black flag with a gold *N* on it. He pushed the flag into the ground. "I take this land in my name! I, Captain Nemo, have come to the South Pole this day, March 21, 1868."

He then turned to the sky. "Good-bye, sun! Sleep! Sleep under this beautiful sea. Let the dark night fall on my new land!"

11 Trapped!

The following morning, the captain took his last look at the Pole. "We will be leaving in a few minutes," he said. "Take another look. The window in the drawing room will be closed."

"Why is that, Captain?" I asked.

"Because it will break if we hit an iceberg," he answered.

I stayed in the drawing room all day. I wanted to write notes about the South Pole. That night I fell asleep thinking about all we had seen on the *Nautilus*.

At three o'clock in the morning, a jarring blow threw me out of bed. The *Nautilus* had run into something!

Ned and Conseil hurried into my room. "Are you all right, Professor?" Ned asked.

"Yes, what happened?" I answered.

"We don't know."

Just then, Captain Nemo came in. "A large iceberg just rolled on top of us," he said.

"Is it dangerous?" I asked.

"It could be," he answered. "We are 1,000 feet from the surface."

The captain took us into the drawing room. He opened the window. "There is ice all around us!" called Ned. "We are trapped!"

"We will see," said Captain Nemo as he left the room.

We felt the submarine climbing up in the water. The top of the ship hit the ice. "There is no escape toward the surface!" Ned cried.

"The captain will find another way," Conseil said.

Then, we felt the *Nautilus* backing up. But after a minute, we stopped again.

The captain came into the room. "Is there any way out of here?" I asked.

"The iceberg closed every opening," the captain answered. "I am afraid we are trapped!"

"Prisoners in a wall of ice!" cried Ned.

"We will try to break that wall," the captain answered. "My men will put on their diving suits. They will look for a thin spot in the iceberg. We will use picks to break through."

"I am as good with a pick as I am with a harpoon. May I help?" asked Ned.

"Yes," the captain answered.

Soon, we could see Ned, Captain Nemo, and some sailors through the window. They looked around the ice. Before long, they began to pick at the ice under the *Nautilus*.

When the men came inside to rest, Captain Nemo talked to us. "The ice under us is 30 feet deep. The water is very cold. We will all take turns working."

Conseil and I put on the diving suits next. We went out with ten sailors. It took most of the day to break off three feet of ice.

Men worked all night long. In the morning, I saw another danger. "Captain, while we pick at the ice, the water is freezing in other places. The sides are closing in the hole. The water around the ship is freezing."

"I know," he said. "We must try to stop it."

He stood deep in thought. Then he said, "I have it! Hot water!"

"Hot water?" I asked.

"Yes! Let's go to the kitchen."

In the kitchen Captain Nemo pointed to some large tanks. "We make our drinking water in these," he said. "The water comes into the ship through this opening in the floor. We will turn the water on and fill the tanks. Then, we will warm it and send the hot water back out into the sea!"

In a few minutes, the water was hot. We sent it out through the opening. Then we filled the tanks with cold water again. We did this over and over.

"It is working!" I said. "The water outside is not freezing any more."

"All we have to think about now is air," said Captain Nemo. "We can live only another day without fresh air."

Each man took his turn picking at the ice. It was hard work, but air in the diving tanks was still good. By now, the air on the submarine was very bad. We were happy to work outside.

When night came, only six feet of ice held us in. The air in the diving tanks was almost gone.

When I woke up the next morning, I felt sick. My head hurt. The room seemed to be turning around. The air was very bad.

Captain Nemo knew we could not cut through the ice in time. "I want all sailors on board," he said. "We will try to break the ice with the *Nautilus!*"

Soon, the *Nautilus* began to move. The submarine hit the ice. "I hear it breaking!" cried Conseil. "We are going to make it!"

At last, we felt the submarine pick up speed. "We have escaped!" cried Ned. "Now we have to get on top of the ice field."

All night long, the *Nautilus* hurried north. We were still under the ice field.

"We will not live until morning," I said. "I am not even strong enough to move my own hand!"

"We are still under 20 feet of ice," Conseil said.

All at once, the *Nautilus* headed toward the surface.

"The captain is going to try to break through the ice!" called Ned.

We felt the ship hit the ice. Then we felt it dive down again. The *Nautilus* did this many times.

At last, we heard a loud noise. The ship began to shake.

"The ice is breaking!" called Conseil.

All at once, the *Nautilus* pushed through the ice. She came to rest at the surface.

Then we heard the banging of the hatch. "The hatch is open!" I cried. "Smell the fresh air!"

12 The Giant Squids

I don't know how we made it through the hatch. Soon, we were sitting on the deck, taking in all the fresh air we could. In a few minutes, we felt better.

"Professor?" Conseil said in a quiet voice. "We are alone up here. Where are the sailors and Captain Nemo?"

"They must still be inside," I answered.

"I wonder why they did not come up," Ned said.

"They have strong wills," I said. "They wait for the air to come to them."

We did not see Captain Nemo or the sailors for weeks after that. All that time, the *Nautilus* traveled from place to place around the sea. The ship did not seem to be going to any one spot.

On March 31, 1868 we came to Cape Horn. The *Nautilus* went deep down into the sea. We traveled north, along the east side of South America. Then the *Nautilus* turned, and we headed for Africa. On April 13, we went toward America again.

We had been prisoners on the *Nautilus* for a long time. We had already traveled 17,000 leagues under the sea. It looked as though our travels would never end.

"We are coming near land again," Ned told us one day. "We almost lost our lives on this submarine. I have had enough! Professor, do you and Conseil want to stay here?"

"No, Ned," I answered. "You are right. We have been here long enough. I have seen all I want to see. Besides, Captain Nemo is not the same man he used to be. We seem to be in his way."

"Then ask him if he will let us go. If he does not plan to, we will escape."

"Give me time to think about it, Ned," I answered. "If we make the captain angry, we will never get away."

We sat down in the drawing room and looked out of the window. We could see giant sea plants growing in the dark water.

"We are now in the West Indies," I said. "The captain has brought us very deep."

"Yes, 5,000 feet under the surface!" said Conseil.

"Why are the plants so big?" asked Ned.

"Some people believe these plants are food for giant sea animals," I answered. "There are old stories telling of giant squids in these waters. The rocks out there would be good hiding places for them."

"Just like your giant whale, Professor?" Ned asked. "The whale that turned out to be a submarine! I will never believe in giant squids!"

"In these stories, Professor," asked Conseil, "were the squids about 30 feet long?"

"That is right," I answered.

"And did they have eight arms?"

"Yes, they did."

"And did they have big eyes, set near the top of their heads?"

"They sure did."

"And did they have a large bill, like a bird's?"

"Yes, Conseil, how did you know?"

"If you will look out the window, Professor, one of them is watching us!"

Ned and I jumped to the window.

"I don't believe it!" called Ned. "A giant squid!"

The monster was pressing against the window.

"Look at all those suction cups," Conseil said. "There must be 250 of them on each arm!"

"And here come more of the monsters," I said. "There must be ten of them out there."

"Listen to them banging on the ship with their bills," said Ned. "For once, I am glad I am inside the *Nautilus*."

Just then, the *Nautilus* stopped and began to roll and shake.

"We have hit something," I said. "The ship is not moving."

A few minutes went by. The squids were climbing all over the window.

Captain Nemo came into the room. We had not seen him since our escape from the ice. He looked tired. He did not talk to us. The captain went to the window and looked at the squids. I went over to him. "There are a lot of them out there," I said.

"Yes, and they are keeping the *Nautilus* from moving. We will have to attack them," he said.

"With harpoons, Captain?" asked Ned.

"And with axes," he answered. "You may help us, Ned. But first, we will bring the *Nautilus* up to the surface."

We all went to the hatch. In a few minutes, the *Nautilus* had floated to the top of the water. Ten sailors armed with axes were ready to begin the attack.

One of the sailors started to open the hatch. But before he could push it open, the door popped off. A giant arm with suction cups came down the steps.

With one blow of his ax, Captain Nemo cut the arm off. It fell to the floor.

Two more arms came through the hatch. They picked a sailor up and pulled him outside.

"Go after him!" cried the captain.

The men ran through the hatch and attacked the squid. It was holding the sailor up in the air. The monster moved away from the ship and went under the water. We heard the sailor cry out. Then he was gone.

We did not have time to think about that poor man. "Over there!" Ned called out. "The squids are climbing on the deck!"

"The arms grow back as soon as I cut them off!" cried Captain Nemo. He was attacking a squid near the hatch.

"Let me try with my harpoon!" cried Ned. "I will hit it between the eyes!"

Just then, the squid knocked Ned down. It was placing its bill over his head. I moved toward my friend, but I was not fast enough to help him. Captain Nemo got to Ned before I did. The captain buried his ax in the monster's mouth. The giant squid slid back.

"You saved my life once," said the captain, turning toward Ned.

"Thank you," answered Ned. "Now you have saved my life."

Ned then jumped up and pushed his harpoon into the giant squid, finishing it off.

The war was over. The squids, cut up and hurt, moved away from the *Nautilus*.

Captain Nemo stood on the deck, looking at the sea. We had won. But we had also lost a man. He would never rest with his brothers in the Coral Kingdom. The captain began to cry.

13 Attack at Land's End

The next ten days must have been hard for the captain. His thoughts were still with the man killed by the squids.

It seemed as if no one was at the wheel of the ship. The *Nautilus* floated where the waves pushed it. At times, we heard strange organ music coming from the drawing room.

"This is our time to escape!" Ned said. "No one watches the decks. The captain comes out of his cabin only to play the organ."

"You are right," I answered. "You make the plans. We will do as you say."

We were near the United States. The wind was strong. It was raining, and the waves were very high.

"I don't think we can escape right now," Ned told us the next day. "But let me say this. We are heading north. I had enough of the South Pole. I will not go to the North Pole!"

"What can we do, Ned?" I asked.

"You must talk with the captain," he answered. "Find out if he will let us go."

"But the captain does not come near us any more," I said.

"Then you must find him," Ned answered.

I went to the captain's cabin. I could hear him inside. I knocked on the door, but he did not answer. I pushed the door. It opened.

Captain Nemo was at his work table. I went over to him. He looked surprised to see me.

"What are you doing here?"

"I want to talk with you, Captain."

"I am busy! Will you not give me the same rights I give you? Will you not give me the right to be alone?"

"Captain, I must talk with you."

"About the sea? Look at this, Professor," he said. "This is a book I have just finished. It tells all I have learned about the sea. It also tells about me. I will keep this book in this box. When our lives end and my ship is gone, it will float to the top. My story will go where the waves carry it."

"I am happy that you are planning to give your learning to the world. My friends and I would be happy to keep it for you. If you will let us go . . ."

"Let you go? I told you when you first came on board, you shall never leave! I will say no more!"

I went back to my cabin. I told Ned and Conseil what the captain had said.

"We must still try to get away. We will make a break for it soon," Ned told us. "I will tell you when it is time."

Wind and waves were strong until the end of May. At that time, Captain Nemo began to run the ship again. The *Nautilus* headed toward England. We could see Land's End from the deck. The ship stayed on top of the water.

For two days, the *Nautilus* traveled in small circles. It was almost as if the captain were looking for something.

The next day, June 1, Captain Nemo came up to the deck. He took a reading of the sun. Then he looked around. About seven miles east of us, we could see a large ship. The ship had no flag.

The captain watched. At last, I heard him say, "This is it!"

Captain Nemo went down through the hatch. I watched as the other ship turned toward the *Nautilus*.

They have spotted us! I thought.

I went into the ship to tell Ned and Conseil. "There is a ship coming toward us!" I cried. "If we can get to them, we will be saved!"

"Wait!" called Conseil. "Do you hear what I hear?"

"Yes!" answered Ned. "The tanks are filling with water. We are going to dive!"

All at once, the *Nautilus* began diving straight down into the sea. At last, we felt her hit bottom. All engines were off.

"She will not stay at the bottom without the engines," I said. "We will float back to the top."

It took almost ten minutes, but the *Nautilus* hit the top. We were met with a loud noise.

"What was that?" I asked.

"A cannon!" answered Ned. "That ship is firing at us!"

The three of us ran up to the deck.

"The ship is only five miles away! We have never been so close to escape!"

"They must have learned that the giant monster is a submarine," I said.

"Commander Farragut heard the ringing sound when I harpooned your giant whale," Ned answered, laughing. "They knew it was not an animal!"

"Is it the *Abraham Lincoln?*" asked Conseil.

"I don't know," I answered. "Even if it is, they don't know we are on board. They will kill us all."

"Let's wave at them," Ned said. "If they see us, they will be careful."

Ned began waving at the ship. Just then, he was knocked to the ground. "Stop that, Mr. Land!" cried the captain. "Do you want me to nail you to the deck before we hit that ship?"

Captain Nemo was very angry. I thought he was going to attack Ned again. But he did not. He turned his angry face toward the attacking ship.

"You know who I am!" he cried. "You hide your colors, but I know you without your flag. Watch, I will show you my colors!"

Captain Nemo went to the front of the ship. He pulled out a black flag, just like the one he planted at the Pole.

Just then a shell hit the *Nautilus.*

"Get out of here!" he called to us. "Get back inside!"

"Captain," I cried, "are you going to attack that ship?"

"Yes, Professor," he answered. "I am going to cut it in two. That is a ship of war. And I am at war with war!" His face was as cold and hard as a stone.

As we went through the hatch, we could hear Captain Nemo calling out. "I am the good! I am the right! You—you who would make war—have killed all that I ever loved! You killed my family, my children, my life. Now, I will kill you!"

Another cannon shell hit the deck of the *Nautilus*. "Hit us! Hit us with your shells!" the captain roared. "Use them up. You will not hurt us. When you run out of shells and your cannons are quiet, we will cut you in two!"

"We must escape!" I cried to my friends.

"Yes," answered Ned. "As soon as we get near the other ship, we will jump into the sea. Captain Nemo will attack from the surface of the water. We may be killed along with the men on the other ship. But we must get away."

We thought Captain Nemo would close in on the other ship and attack. But no. He moved away! He was playing a waiting game. The captain would attack in his own good time.

Night came, but the ship of war was still far away. Everything on the *Nautilus* was quiet. I went up to the deck. Captain Nemo was still there. The captain was standing watch. I stood on the deck with him all night. At last, it began to get light. I could see the other ship. It was now only about two miles away. *We can swim that far*, I thought.

I went through the hatch to get my friends. They were in their room, waiting for me.

"It is time," I said.

Just then, we heard a banging sound.

"The hatch is closing!" cried Ned.

"The tanks are filling with water!"

"It is too late!" Conseil cried. "We are diving again!"

The *Nautilus* picked up speed. It was moving toward the other ship. "The captain is attacking!" Ned said.

A few minutes went by. All at once, we hit the other ship. We were knocked to the floor. The *Nautilus* kept moving. We hurried into the drawing room to see what was happening.

There, in front of the window, stood Captain Nemo. He was laughing as he watched the other ship. The *Nautilus* had cut it in two, sending it to the bottom of the sea. The captain watched men from the ship trying to swim for their lives.

Soon, the sea was quiet. Pieces of the ship of war fell to the bottom. Everyone on board had been killed. When it was all over, Captain Nemo turned. Without a word, he left the room.

I followed him to his cabin. On the far wall were pictures of a woman and two small children.

Captain Nemo looked at them and fell to the floor, crying.

14 The Maelstrom

After this attack, the window stayed closed. All the lights were shut off. Everything was dark and quiet inside the *Nautilus*. Once in a while, we heard organ music.

We traveled at great speeds for many days. We stayed under the water most of the time. It seemed as if Captain Nemo was running away.

At last, the lights came on again. We were heading north, toward the Arctic Circle. The *Nautilus* now traveled on top of the water.

I could not sleep well at night. All I could think about was what Captain Nemo had done. All those men killed! For what?

Early one morning, Ned came to see me. "Professor, we are going to escape!" he said.

"When?"

"When night falls," he answered. "No one is watching the deck. This morning I saw land."

"What is your plan, Ned?" I asked.

"Meet us at the small boat on deck at ten o'clock. The wind is strong, but I will row 20 miles if I have to."

"I will be there, Ned," I answered. "I will be there."

I sat alone in my cabin all day. We were afraid to be together. We did not want to give away our plan.

I put on my heavy clothes. I brought all my notes together. Then I sat and waited.

A little after nine o'clock that night, I heard music. It was coming from the drawing room. Captain Nemo was playing the organ again.

I must walk through that room to get out! I thought. *He will see me!*

I waited until just before ten o'clock. The captain was still playing. *I must try! They are waiting for me!*

I tried to be very quiet. I went down the hall. Then I opened the door to the drawing room.

It was dark. Captain Nemo had his back to me.

Step by step, I moved across the room. I was careful not to make a sound.

At last, I got to the far door. Just as I was going to open it, the music stopped. Captain Nemo got up! He started to walk toward me! Did he see me? I did not know.

The man was deep in thought. His eyes were red. Deep circles were under them. Then I heard him say something to himself: "My God! Enough! *Enough!*"

Afraid that he would see me, I pushed the door open. I hurried through the other rooms and up to the hatch. It was already open. Ned and Conseil helped me up.

"Let's go!" I cried.

Ned started to push us off. Then we heard voices inside the ship. "Have they found out about us?" called Ned. He pulled out his knife.

"No," I said. "They are crying 'The Maelstrom!' The Maelstrom is a whirlpool that takes ships to the bottom of the sea. Few ships escape! We must be near it now."

Just then, we started to turn in circles. The whirlpool was pulling the *Nautilus* under the sea!

"This cannot happen now," cried Ned. "Not just when we are escaping!"

The circling water was strong. It pulled us from the *Nautilus*. It threw our small boat into the sea like a stone.

My head hit the side of the small boat. The blow knocked me out. Everything went black. I do not know what happened after that.

And so, our travels under the sea ended. How we escaped the Maelstrom, I don't know. When I came to, I was in a home in a small fishing town. Ned and Conseil were beside me.

It is in the home of these fishing people that I am writing my story. Will the world believe me? Will they believe that we traveled 20,000 leagues under the sea? I don't know.

My friends and I wonder what happened to the *Nautilus*. Did she escape the Maelstrom? Or did Captain Nemo plan to take her there? One day, will waves wash a small box up on land? Will the box with Captain Nemo's book inside ever be found? Will Captain Nemo's strange story ever be told? Only the sea can answer these questions. The sea, and only the sea . . .